The RECOVERY ROOM

The Woman
Behind the
Masks
of Trauma

Regina L. Jones

The Recovery Room
The Woman Behind the Masks of Trauma
Regina L. Jones

To contact the author:
Reginajones7777@gmail.com

Library of Congress Control Number: 2026911147
ISBN (Print): 978-1-966561-47-7
ISBN (eBook): 978-1-966561-48-4

Published by:

Mary Ethel

Mary Ethel Eckard
Frisco, Texas

All Scripture quotations are taken from the Holy Bible, King James Version, found on the public domain.

DEDICATION

To all the women and men who suffer in silence from sexual abuse inside the home. Please allow me, with the help of leading through the Holy Spirit, to be your voice until you feel comfortable enough to share your story, your pain, and your hardships. Just know that you are not alone, and there is hope in Jesus Christ.

I pray for your healing, deliverance and freedom from bondage, in the name of Jesus.

ACKNOWLEDGEMENTS

Thanks to:

God. And to my Lord and Savior, Jesus Christ.

My husband, Deacon Leo Jones, Sr., for allowing me to lean on him and for helping me to know that I am more than enough.

My children, Gina L. Jiminez and Jasmine C. Jones, for forgiving me all the times I wasn't there.

My cousin-in-law, Lorraine Pernell, for constantly pushing me to put my life on paper.

Pastor J.R. Gatlin and First Lady C. Gatlin of New Life Church of God in Christ, for encouraging me when I wanted to give up. This is the place where God delivered me, set me free from my past, and emotional healing began.

All praise be unto God!

Contents

Preface

At a very early age, I was a lonely and confused girl, not really knowing what was happening to me or whether it was right or wrong. I didn't have the knowledge, or anything else, for that matter. But I do remember at two years old being introduced to a routine that had been given to me. And I knew that if I wouldn't follow through with it, then I would suffer the consequences of being whipped. Little did I know that God would use my "went-throughs" as a testimony so that you, too, can receive your breakthrough.

Please allow me, through the Holy Spirit, to be your voice until you feel comfortable sharing your story. Just know you are not alone and there is hope through Jesus Christ.

Humbly submitted,
Your sister in Christ,
Regina L. Jones

Introduction

There have been times when all I knew was pain. No matter how hard I tried to fix it, by ignoring, masking, or suppressing it, there was still pain. I never understood why one had to go through life experiencing such pain. I didn't realize at the time that my pain would reveal my purpose: to use it to set someone else free, to honor and bring glory to God. Isaiah 53:11, *"By His stripes we are healed."* I began to pray, "Lord, heal me from the inside out!"

As I share my story, may you see that God was with me all the time. Even as a little girl at the age of two, I knew there was a sense of God's presence. In Isaiah 61:3, He said He would *"bestow on them a crown of beauty instead of ashes, the oil of joy instead of mourning, and a garment of praise instead of a spirit of heaviness, that we might be called trees of righteousness."*

I am a living testimony that we can overcome unexpected and unwanted difficulty forced upon us. As we heal through our story and speak it to others, I pray that our testimony will lead them to their own recovery!

Dear reader, just know that you are not alone! There is hope in Jesus Christ.

CHAPTER 1

A Confused Little Girl

WHEN I WAS TWO YEARS old, my dad started fondling me through my wet and soggy diaper. When he heard some background noise, he quickly pulled his hand away. I walked out of the room where he was and hurried to my grandmother's house across the highway. I remember it like it was yesterday!

As the years went by, I began to learn that I wasn't the only one being abused. It was me and my other three sisters and two youngest brothers. You see, I am the youngest of seventeen children. Nine daughters and eight sons. We lived in Denison, Texas, and this is where the abuse began.

In 1976, I was around 8-1/2. We moved to Lancaster, California, where the abuse got worse. My father began to drink more and more! He was an alcoholic to the core. He would go on drinking binges to make up for the times he didn't drink. He was a mean, hateful drunk, but he wouldn't mess with us when he was drinking. I later learned that most of his drinking came from his guilt and shame he would deal with after abusing us. He would apologize for his actions afterward, thinking we would be okay after he did. After all, we were just kids.

I saw him as my father and thought this must be a normal things for children to go through. After his apology, I would answer, "It's okay daddy. I forgive you." Then I would give him a bear hug with joy! But then he got bolder with his actions. He switched it up on me.

He went from molesting me to having me and my siblings do different sexual acts on each other. We were afraid that if we didn't comply to what he wanted, he would make us get a switch from the back yard and he would use it to beat us. This was a horrible, disgusting time and I felt so degraded. When I saw my sisters cry about this, I knew it was not normal! It got worse when he started having me and my sisters do things to each other. My two youngest brothers would watch with him, as they fondled themselves. Afterward, once Dad was pleased, he would tell us to get up, do our homework, or clean the house.

I was totally confused! Where was my mom? She was there the whole time. I would tell her about what Dad was doing, my older siblings would tell her, and she would turn the other cheek. At this particular time, Dad would not do this in front of her, but she knew.

This went on every week, four and five times a week. It got so bad that my brothers would try to come into our room without my dad. The evil spirit that ruled my father had come into my brothers! The Bible says in Ephesians 6:12, *"For we do not wrestle against flesh and blood; but against principalities, against powers, against the rulers of the darkness of this age, against spiritual wickedness."*

Being the youngest, I intended to follow easily. Whatever I saw my sisters and brothers do is what I did. Walking around, sucking my thumb, being confused about my childhood. I didn't know what was right or wrong. I played with my toys and dolls for a while, but wasn't happy doing that, knowing that any second, I could be called into the house for more sexual abuse.

Then, the voice of fear called my name. It was my brother. "Regina, come in the house. Mama is sick and we need to get her to the hospital." I cried and ran into the house. My mom was hurting, crying, and moaning. The ambulance came and took her away. I thought she would never come back, but she did. But she was slowly dying, and my dad used this for his good.

Mom could barely walk. She had a hospital bed in the living room, a wheelchair, and a potty chair. She could no longer care for herself, and I thought, "NOOOOOO." She was my only hope for this abuse to come to an end. Maybe one day she would stop daddy from hurting us; she would believe us; she would come to our rescue. But that wasn't going to happen. She was suffering from kidney failure and had a short leash on life.

CHAPTER 2

Curiosity Sets In

AS I GREW OLDER, I began to ask questions about what was going on with me to my sisters and brothers. I wanted to know if this was normal, because I felt disgusted. My life and my childhood were a terrible place, and I didn't want any part of it. But, for some reason, I still had hope.

When I was alone, I could feel a presence. This presence was God! I knew at an early age that I didn't want His presence to ever leave me, and without it, I knew nothing was worthwhile. But with Him, everything could have a meaning, purpose, and effectiveness.

"In your presence is fullness of joy."
Psalm 16:11

When I realized that I wasn't alone during these struggles, I felt a sense of peace. But it didn't stop the abuse that was still taking place: mentally, emotionally, and sexually.

One day I was called into my parents' bedroom to lie down and watch television with them. I knew the sexual abuse was about to take place again. As I laid between my biological mom and dad, he would try and penetrate me with his private part, and my mother would pretend to read the newspaper or watch television. For the first time, I began to get angry. Why wasn't she stopping him? Why wasn't she protecting me? He was hurting me. I know she heard my weeping and sobbing, and I know she saw the tears rolling down my face. But she just laid there.

This was the beginning of my issues with anger, trust, abandonment, and rejection. But even in this time, I knew I wasn't alone. I wasn't knowledgeable to the extent to know God's Word like I do now, but I knew He was with me, even in those issues.

"Keep your heart with diligence, for out of it flows the issues of life."
Proverbs 4:23 NKJV

I was still an angry little girl when my mother died. As we moved to Washington where my stepdad (the father of some of my older siblings) lived, I had a sense of release from all the trauma that was taking place. Little did I know that I still had to deal with all of the issues as I became older. But in my mind, I was free! When I moved to Washington, my dad moved back home to live with his mom in Denison, Texas, and I didn't have to endure anymore pain or misery from him anymore. Or so I thought.

As I started my new life in Washington, I was so excited. But still, I had to deal with the trauma in my mind. I didn't trust anyone, especially men, so even when I was free, I wasn't free. I didn't know how to process the fear, the pain, the hurt that was deeply rooted in my mind.

I was enrolled in school, and things began to go up from there. I made new friends and began to enjoy life as a kid. But eventually, I began to isolate from my friends, one by one, and they began to call me names like "Weirdo," "Dumb," and "Stupid." I would swing by myself and listen to the turmoil that was playing back and forth in my mind.

One of the most hurtful things was when I realized they all knew what was going on inside my home. They began to whisper things like: "That's her. She's the little girl my parents were talking about." Turmoil began to take its place, and I became an angry and sad little girl.

I stayed in Washington for about four years. Afterward, me and two of my sisters moved back to Texas to live with my grandmother and my father. But for some reason, after just a little while, my sisters moved back to Washington and left me with the same man I had been free from. The spirit of loneliness and fear crept back in!

I had hopes of being with my grandmother, because I knew she wouldn't allow anything to happen to me. She would protect me, so I thought. I was thirteen years old and my life as a teenager was about to begin.

CHAPTER 3

Teenage Prostitution

AS I BEGAN TO EXPLORE drug use at age 13, I made some friends at Junior High School. I was in seventh grade, and I was excited to meet new people. I met three or four friends and life began to look up. We would hang out at recess, walk home together, and talk girl stuff, laughing and enjoying ourselves.

As I got closer to home, I became quiet. My friends asked questions like, "Why come every time we get ready to depart from each other, the countenance on your face changes?" As I walked up the front stairs to the house, I looked around for my grandmother, yelled out for her, and she responded, "I'm in the kitchen, baby." I walked toward the kitchen and, when I entered, there was my father. A big knot of fear came up in my throat.

After we ate, my grandmother would take a nap and I would get ready to do my homework in my room. Then my father would enter my room, with his finger over his mouth telling me to be quiet, and I knew the routine was starting over again. I began to cry, and he ignored me— as usual.

After he finished molesting me, he would get up to leave, and I would go to the bathroom to clean up. I sat there crying and weeping until I pulled myself together. The routine was back.

I continued to go to school, and that's where I was introduced to Mary Jane (weed). This was my new best friend. It made me calm and at peace with what was going on inside the home. But the scripture tells us:

> *"They have treated the wound of my people carelessly, saying Peace, Peace; when there is no peace."*
> Jeremiah 6:14 KJV

As I began to get high, my grades began to fall. Between getting high, trying to complete the seventh grade, and coping with what was going on inside the home, I ended up quitting school. My dad didn't care nor did my grandmother. This was another routine in my life- being hooked on marijuana. My grandmother and Dad both knew I was smoking. They told me to support my own habit. She was a smoker and a drinker; my dad just drank.

I remember seeing different men come to my grandmama's house. They would follow her into her bedroom. Afterwards, she would call out for me and my dad to come to the screened-in porch where she would give us some money. I finally asked her why these men came over all the time, and that's when the teaching began. She taught me how to sleep for money. She gave me some of her clients, but I had to give her most of the money. She gave me enough for my habit.

I was spiraling out of control. I began to get my own clients to earn money for my drug use. And before I knew it, I started trying other drugs. Black mollies, yellow mollies, powder, crack cocaine – anything to keep me numb from feeling anything that wasn't comfortable feeling. I was living a life of misery, drowning in my own sin and sinful ways.

The "A" clause of Romans 6:23 says, *"For the wages of sin is death."* That's what it felt like. I didn't want to go home and didn't want to be in the streets. I was merely existing. I didn't know how to process my feelings, emotions, anger, or bitterness, so I started acting out in ways I had never done. I started getting into fights with people. Again, the whole community knew about the abuse, but no one reached out to show me how to handle the situation. People were in their own world, I guess, but at the same time, I was scared and ashamed to tell anyone. I was stuck between a rock and a hard place.

When I was 14, I got pregnant and was forced to marry the father. We were married on August 4. We separated two weeks later because he wasn't any help, he was an alcoholic, and he was physically abusive. Something I was very familiar with. I was free to go back to what I was used to, which was working the streets.

Imagine that: a little girl having a baby. I had her but didn't raise her by myself. One of my older sisters helped, as well as my grandmother and my stepmom. I didn't know what to do and where to start trying to be a mother. In reality, how can you teach or be someone that you've never experienced or had? Eventually, I let my friend keep my little girl until she was about five.

"As a dog returneth to his vomit, so a fool returneth to his folly."
Proverbs 26:11

As I returned to the streets, I also returned to the stores to steal and support my habits. That's the first time I was arrested. I went to jail and was released, but I continued to repeat that cycle. After so many times, my misdemeanors turned into a felony where I had to do time in prison. The courts enhanced my stealing to robbery because I tried to run out of the store. They gave me eight years prison time in the Texas Department of Corrections.

That's where I found the time to think about my life. After serving my time, I was out on parole. I went back to the block where people were partying. Familiar faces began to welcome me home by feeding me illegal drugs so they could get me hooked all over again.

CHAPTER 4

The Rescue

AS I BEGAN MY LATE teenage years, I was introduced to powder from cocaine and I spiraled from worse to worse. I started going to Sherman, a town ten miles away from Denison. I loved Sherman due to the clubs and little juke box joints. They had more nightlife, malls, and drugs.

I was introduced to crack cocaine around the age of 19 and became the town's biggest thief to support my habit of drug use. Between prostitution and stealing from stores, there was no stopping me. The enemy himself was sifting me like wheat. I felt like Peter in Luke 22:31,

> *"And He said, 'Simon, Simon, behold Satan asked for you, that he may sift you as wheat.'"*

My drug use began to escalate on another level. Crack was my new friend, my go-to when unwanted feelings and emotions arose from being the victim of sexual abuse. My one-thousand dollars a day drug habit had me sleeping in cars, trucks, whenever I slept, as I waited on the stores to open so I could get my next high.

The devil had worn out my body with prostitution, and no one wanted my service anymore. I was a mess. I was living on the streets, and I was so tired but, at no point would I stop this cycle. At least, not until I was ready!

One evening while I was on the block, a place everyone flocked to drink, play pool, sell or even use drugs, a church was doing a street revival. Right in the midst of the block, I overheard someone say this:

"God can heal you from all the pain and
hurt that you're going through.
He loves you. He can be whatever you need Him to be!"

As I was listening, a sense of God's presence began to surround me, just like it did when I was a little girl. But I ran from His voice, His tugging, and continued to pick up where I left off.

"And one cried unto another and said,
'Holy, Holy, Holy, is the Lord of hosts; the
whole earth is full of His glory.'"
Isaiah 6:3

Then one day, I met a man named Leo. A really nice man, a different type of man than those I was used to knowing. He asked if he could take me to dinner and I asked, "What do you mean? What do you want from me? How much are you willing to give me?" I knew he wanted something from me. After all, these were the only men I was used to dealing with.

Leo looked confused and said, "I don't want nothing from you. I just asked you one question. Do you want to or not?" I answered, "Yes, but you will need to take me home to get cleaned up." He took me home and I asked him to give me a few minutes. But as I was getting ready, the spirit of fear began to set in because I was still paranoid about this nice man being something and someone that I wasn't used to. So again, I ran.

I went in the front door and snuck out the back door of the house, leaving him sitting in the car, waiting on me. All a while, I was down the street partying at the club. As I walked out of the club, he was walking in and looked at me. "Look, Lady, I don't know what's wrong with you, but I feel like I need to tell you that I was sent here for you." He began to tell me that he was a backslider and was running from the Lord. Leo said he was in the process of getting a divorce. This was another part of how God opened my heart and eyes to Christ.

"For my thoughts are not your thoughts,
Neither are your ways my ways, saith the Lord.
For as the heavens are higher than the earth,
So are my ways higher than your ways
And my thoughts than your thoughts."
Isaiah 55:8-9

God was breaking me free from the norm of life, but it wasn't easy. As I tried to accept this new part of life with this nice man, I was still an addict, a scorned little girl within, and my thought pattern was still bound to my past. I lied to him when he asked my age and told him I was 24. Even in that, I thought it was strange that I would lie about my age. Later I learned that he would not have dated me if I told him I was 18 because he had a daughter that age. When he found out

I was lying, he was upset, but within a respectable way. And I kept asking myself, what's going on with this type of man? What does he see in me?

We had already fallen in love, but I was still a junkie. We moved in together and we made a go of it. I told him that I was married and he was okay with it as long as it wouldn't be a problem. I told him I was a stone drug addict. Sooner or later, he began to use drugs, too. Then I got busted again for stealing and went back to prison.

But this time, love waited on me. He would visit me and put money on my account so I could have extras. While I was in prison, he got us a two bedroom place to stay, which was better than what we were living in. He got himself cleaned up and, when I got out, we started life over again. This time, I was determined to stay clean.

CHAPTER 5

Turning Another Leaf

LEO TOLD ME THAT GOD was dealing with him. There were many nights he wasn't able to sleep because he was running from God. He told me that he was a backslider.

> *"'Turn, O backsliding children,' saith the Lord*
> *'For I am married unto you:*
> *And I will take you one of a city*
> *And two of a family*
> *And I will bring you to Zion.'"*
> Jeremiah 3:14

As Leo told me about his backsliding, memories of feeling God's presence flooded my mind. I told him everything that he deserved to know about me. I was a victim of every kind of abuse imaginable. I knelt down and cried, feeling overwhelmed while telling him about my past of being molested by my parents. I said, "So if you see me pulling back from you or even having an emotional outburst and not trusting you, I don't mean it." He looked me in my uncontrollable, teary eyes and said, "We can get through this together. You are more than enough!"

As I realized I was becoming a different person, I still had that tugging of my old lifestyle. The different mindsets, my flesh longed for drugs, and the fast life was still gripping me. But God had a ram in the bush! I learned I was pregnant. Yes, pregnant! After ten years, I was pregnant.

This was a blessing in disguise. I thought, "Well, I'm not using or going back to that old lifestyle." But the grip of the enemy, Satan himself, pulled me back in for two more months. But God gave me mercy even though I wasn't serving Him. I quit, by the grace of God, cold turkey. I didn't want my daughter to come into this world addicted. I went and got my first daughter, Gina, from my brother, who released her to me. After the baby was born, we were a family of four!

One Friday, a witness of Jesus Christ saw me outside and came to witness to me. She asked if I would like to be her guest that night at church. For some reason, I answered, "Yes." She picked me up and we went to a church in Greenville, Texas, called Pilgrim Tabernacle Church of Deliverance. I listened attentively as the man of God preached from Mark 5:1-5. It seemed he was talking to me, telling me that I didn't have to leave the same way I came. And I didn't.

At the end of the service, I went to the altar, and the power of God slayed me in the spirit. When I came to, I jumped up and down, shouting, "I'm free! I'm free!" I asked the Lord to forgive me for all the wrong I had done. I asked Jesus to fill me with the power of the Holy Ghost with the evidence of speaking in an unknown tongue.

"That if thou shalt confess with thy mouth the Lord Jesus, and shalt believe in thine heart that God hath raised Him from the dead, thou shalt be saved. For with the heart, man believeth unto righteousness and with the mouth, confession is made unto salvation."
Romans 10:9-10

"But ye shall receive power. After that, the Holy Ghost is come upon you, and ye shall be my witnesses unto me both in Jerusalem, and in all Judea, and in Samaria, and unto the uttermost part of the earth."
Acts 1:8

As I went home from church, the chains had been broken off. I could feel it! I knew I was different and that I didn't see anything the same way as before I gave my heart to the will of God.

I went to bed and drifted off to sleep. About two hours later, I was awakened by a voice saying 1 Corinthians 6:9. I immediately got up and looked up the verse the Holy Spirit spoke, because I was ignorant; unlearned to the Word of God.

"Know ye not that the unrighteous shall not inherit the kingdom of God? Be not deceived: neither fornicators, nor idolaters, nor adulterers."
1 Corinthians 6:9

Conviction fell on me. I knew something had to be done so that I was not living in sin. I woke up the man beside me and said, "Leo, Leo! I can't sleep with you anymore. I am committing adultery and you are fornicating." I asked, "Which one do you want? The couch or the bed. It doesn't matter to me, but we cannot do this because this is not pleasing in the eyesight of God."

He answered, "I understand. I already knew it because I am a backslider and already knew it was wrong." He didn't fight me on this. I told him that I would find my husband and get a divorce, and he told me he would sleep on the couch until we could be married.

God gave us every grace and avenue in finding my husband. I got the divorce and then married my new husband, Mr. Deacon Leo Jones, Sr. He committed his life to the Lord, and to this day, we have been together a total of 43 years, 29 of those years being done the "right" way. All because we wanted to please our Lord and Savior, Jesus Christ.

CHAPTER 6

The Revealing of the Woman Behind the Masks

AS I BEGAN TO GROW in God's Word, I realized there were still wounds that I hadn't totally surrendered to God. This gave the enemy a portal to creep back in. Slowly, over a period of time, I began to turn a blind eye to what was really taking place.

I was in the will of God and still missed Him by holding on to regrets, past failures, past traumas, unforgiveness, etc. I began slipping away more and more, and just like that, I turned my back on God. Again. But not in the same way nor the same drugs. This time, the schemes of Satan were prescription pills to pull me back. I was bound on every opiate medication on the market. I had a surgical procedure and was prescribed opiates, and I was hooked. My addiction was so bad that I began to buy them off the streets.

We moved from Leonard, TX to Bonham, TX. I was working and functioning like normal people, but I was still hiding, even though I was out in the open. Leo showed me love through it all. I was in more turmoil than I had ever been.

"When the unclean spirit is gone out of a man, he walketh through dry places, seeking rest, and findeth none. Then he saith, 'I will return into my house from whence I came out;' and when he is come, he findeth it empty, swept, and garnished. Then goeth he, and taketh himself seven other spirits more wicked than himself, and they enter in and dwell there: and the last state of that man is worse than the first. Even so shall it be also unto this wicked generation."
Matthew 12:43-45

I started partying, drinking, listening to all kinds of music that would pump me up higher and higher. But I was getting tired. Tired of the lifestyle, the chase of the opiates. The enemy was trying to kill me, and I gave him full charge to do just that.

"Know ye not, that to whom ye yield yourselves servants to obey, his servants ye are to whom ye obey; whether of sin unto death, or of obedience unto righteousness?"
Romans 6:16

One afternoon, Leo and my youngest child, Jasmine, asked me to come grocery shopping with them. But I was jonesing too badly, aching, and my mind was wandering all over the place, trying to figure out where I would get money to get a fix. I told Leo and Jasmine to go ahead without me. As they walked out the door, I turned the television off so I could think better. But I couldn't think straight.

Suddenly, conviction set in from God, and it seemed that I could literally feel something fall off my face, and I began to talk to God. I fell in my living room floor and began to weep and cry out to God. I prayed, "I'm tired and I want help. I don't want to live like this anymore. If you could just help me; I know that you're real because I've once tasted the goodness of you." I told Him I was sorry and asked Him to please forgive me. And He did just that.

I checked myself into a rehab in Dallas, Texas and stayed there until they told me I could stay as an inpatient if I needed longer. I answered, "No, I'm good. God has me now."

I started going to New Life Church of God in Christ in Bonham, under the leadership of Pastor J.R. Gatlin and First Lady Criselle Gatlin. This is the place where God delivered me and set me free from my past. This is the place where my emotional healing began.

All praises be unto God!

CHAPTER 7

Learning to Forgive God's Way

"And forgive us our debts as we forgive our debtors."
"For if ye forgive men their trespasses, your heavenly Father will also forgive you."
Matthew 6:12 and 6:14

I WAS CLEANING UP THE church one day, singing and praising the Lord while I dusted and swept the kitchen. Then I heard the Lord say, "Go into the sanctuary." I paused for a minute or two but then I kept on sweeping. Again, He said, "Go into the sanctuary."

I knew it was the Lord, because instead of me going in there, I went to clean the bathrooms. The Lord's presence and I were the only ones in the church. As I began to clean the toilets, conviction began to set in where I couldn't override it anymore. I knew deliverance was about to take place, I just didn't know what type of deliverance. So, I went into the sanctuary and grabbed my tissues and a trash can.

As I sat at the altar, I said, "Here I am Lord." And these are the words He spoke to me: "Daughter, you're going to have to forgive your father!" I replied, "Oh Lord, I forgave him. Remember I told him it was okay after he molested me. Remember, Lord?"

He replied, "Yes, daughter, you did. But you forgave him because he was your father and not because of the acts he committed." I began to tell the Lord, "Yes, I will forgive him." I began to cry out to the Lord and I said, "I forgive him, Lord." I also voiced it to my father that I forgave him, even though he had passed away; he died when I was in prison.

I didn't know I held in unforgiveness, but when I let go of that pain, it felt like a brick house was lifted off my shoulders. I was happy and excited, because my desire was to make my heavenly Father pleased with my life and to give him all the glory that He deserves!

"If the Son therefore shall make you free, ye shall be free indeed."
John 6:36

But He wasn't done yet! As I began to gather my tissues and trashcan to leave the sanctuary, He spoke to me again and said, "Now you have to forgive your mother." I was angry and blurted out, "Noooooo way, God. I'm not doing that one. Nope. I'm not!" And as I started crying profusely, the Lord told me to call Missionary Edna Wilson, a mother of the church. She answered on the second ring. I asked her if she could come to the church and she immediately knew something was wrong. She hung up the phone and came.

I unlocked the door for her, and she followed me into the sanctuary. I sat back down at the altar, mad and angry. She looked at me but never said a word. She just waited until I was ready to tell her what I needed. I looked up at her and said, "God wants me to forgive my mother, and I told Him I wasn't doing that." She still said nothing.

I yelled out, "She was supposed to protect me and she didn't! She was my mother and she knew. She was laying there and let him have his way with me. On top of that, she abandoned me! She had the audacity to die on me! I'm not forgiving her."

She said, "Sister Jones, you're going to have to forgive her so you can be free and so God can use you to help other people such as yourself. Let God free you, heal you, and mend your broken heart." When she said that, I hollered in a loud voice; it sounded like Tarzan when he swung from vine to vine. God healed me of so many things when I forgave my mother! I didn't realize I had all the emotional anger and bitterness toward my mom until I released it all. I was free indeed.

"He healeth the broken in heart, and bindeth up their wounds."
Psalm 147:3

It was my turn to begin to live for the Lord, saved, sanctified, and filled with His power of the Holy Ghost. I was joyful, doing what I could to lift the kingdom of God.

One day I was in prayer in my home and God put my loving children before my face. When I asked him what was wrong, He answered, "You need to ask them to forgive you for not being there for them when they needed you the most." I immediately said, "Yes, Lord."

I continued to pray and asked God to give me wisdom in how to do that because I didn't want to go to them with excuses of why I wasn't there. God answered my prayer. I asked them both if we could have a family meeting. We would have these from time to time, just in case one had something they needed to talk about. They would talk and we would listen, and if we could help in any way, then we would. Other times, they just needed a listening ear.

They came to our house, and we sat at the dining room table. I asked them to please forgive me for not being the mother they deserved. I was in prison three times, leaving them with their father, my husband. They both forgave me and we cried. They told me how they felt and I let them have their say. After all, that was the least I could do.

They are both in my life to this day. Hallelujah. I have one grandson by Gina, and I have two grandchildren by Jasmine, a granddaughter and a grandson. All praise belongs to God, the God of restoration.

"He will turn the hearts of the parents to their children and the hearts of the children to their parents."
Malachi 4:6

Today, I'm living my life to the fullest in Jesus Christ. I'm still married to my husband, Mr. Deacon Leo Jones, Sr. and we still live in Bonham, Texas, a small town in North Texas. Both of our children and our three grandchildren live here as well.

I'm fully committed to God's will, which is to serve Him with a clean and pure heart. We are fully committed members of Full Gospel Holy Temple in Denison, Texas, under the leadership of Pastor Emmanuel Johnson and First Lady Charlene Evangelist Johnson, where we are being taught the unadulterated Word of God. My husband, children, and I truly and humbly thank God that they lead by example, teaching us that Jesus forgives, saves, and fills us with His Spirit.

Pastor Johnson and First Lady Johnson, you both are the model parents that I desired to have growing up. Thank you for all the times that you showed the love of God to me through your saved, sanctified life, to this day! Keep shining for Jesus, keep proclaiming His love and suffering, but most of all, proclaiming salvation to a dying world. We, the Jones family, love you both dearly.

CHAPTER 8

Still Learning to Forgive in God's Way

AS I WAS LEARNING TO forgive God's way, I forgot about one person I needed to forgive. It was vital that I forgive her because I couldn't move forward until I did.

That person was me. I didn't realize I needed to forgive myself. God showed me that I held myself hostage to all the mistakes and all the wrong choices I had made over the years. I was holding myself in bondage. You see, God had forgiven me, I had forgiven others, and I asked others to forgive me. I thought that was it. But that was far from the truth! I still felt trapped in different areas of my walk with God, and I knew I wanted to be totally free. That meant I had to seek God on how to forgive myself. He showed me this Scripture:

"Howbeit when he, the spirit of truth, is come,
he will guide you into all truth."
John 16:13

I began to listen to the Spirit of God on how to get free. He gave me different Scriptures to let me know it was okay to forgive myself. It was like He was trying to explain to me that I hadn't shed blood, and the same price He paid to forgive everyone else was also enough for me. I must admit, this was the hardest part of my forgiveness stage. Forgiving myself.

Here I was eager to make sure everyone was good, but when it came to me, I felt I wasn't worthy of forgiving myself. I had so many triggers to work through, like seeing an ad about parental neglect of children or seeing a piece of gravel that reminded me of my drug use. When I saw a movie about an unfaithful spouse, I felt unworthy to release myself from the past traumas and past deeds.

But the Lord let me know that I was putting me before Him in doing that. Staying stuck in the past after He had forgiven me was degrading to His deity, His divinity, and most of all, His shedding of blood for the remission of ALL MY SINS. He wanted me to realize that He had paid the ultimate price so that I could have complete forgiveness!

"As far as the east is from the west,
so far hath he removed our transgressions from us."
Psalm 103:12

Even now, I have to continue to speak the Word of God over my life. I use different Scriptures concerning my complete forgiveness. I also take it by faith, talk by faith, walk by faith, and live faith in my life through God's Holy Word. You see, the enemy never stops. He'll always be lurking behind the scenes to try and remind us of our past. He'll always remind other people of our past, too. Because just like God works through people, so does the devil. He'll leave us for a season, just like he did Jesus. But we already know that we have the victory through our Lord and Savior, Jesus Christ.

"And when the devil ended all the temptation,
he departed from him for a season."
Luke 4:13

The Three Gates

That's why it's important, necessary, and crucial that we watch what we feed our spirit man. We have to watch our *eye gate, ear gate, and mouth gate.* What we see and put before our eyes will represent as a portal for the enemy to use against us. Stay studying God's Word and pray often.

Also be careful what you watch on television. Please! Anything that reminds you of your past that has a grip on you is not of God. You already know that it's from the enemy.

Be extra careful what you listen to whether it be different conversations, music, etc., that cause raw emotions from your past to creep in. Listen to some Gospel music, listen to the voice of God by allowing the Holy Ghost (Spirit) to bring to your remembrance what God says about you.

Be careful what you say to others, but more importantly to yourself. Speak good things. Speak life into your mind and your heart. Words bring either life or destruction. Negative words or thoughts will bring negative consequences.

"Death and life are in the power of the tongue:
and they that love it shall eat the fruit thereof."
Proverbs 18:21

Remember to keep your mind on the good things God says about you.

"Finally, brethren, whatsoever things are true, whatsoever things are honest, whatsoever things are just, whatsoever things are pure, whatsoever things are lovely, whatsoever things are of good report; if there be any virtue, and if there be any praise, think on these things."
Philippians 4:8

CHAPTER 9

The Trusting Process

AS I CONTINUED TO WALK in my new way of life with Christ Jesus, I realized I couldn't lean to my own way of thinking and doing things anymore. I had been conjuring up my own ways of surviving by the ways of the world. It was hard to do this thing called trust.

"Trust in the Lord with all thine heart; and
lean not unto thine own understanding.
In all they ways acknowledge him and he shall direct thy path."
Proverbs 3 :5-6

But how could I just give up all the ways just like that? I mean, who trusts someone that much? Everyone I had put my trust in failed me and took my trust and love for granted. They saw my vulnerability and used it against me. Sometimes people would tell me what I wanted to hear so they could get what they needed from me. Then they would hang me out to dry until they needed me again.

I remember one time when my faith in God was tested by learning to trust Him in a significant way. I was blessing someone with my time, efforts, and just all around doing a good deed. The enemy tried to twist my blessing into a curse where police were involved. I knew I was innocent but the fear of my past life crept back in. Remember now: I had been to prison three times, so I was already a three time loser in society. I called my husband, Deacon Jones, and began to tell him the issue at hand. Sometimes as children of God, we need some reinforcement to touch and agree.

"Again I say until you that if two of you shall agree on Earth as touching anything they shall ask, it shall be done for them of my Father which is in Heaven."
Matthew 28:19

Deacon Jones answered the phone, and I began to tell him about the situation at hand. He said to me, "Let's pray RIGHT NOW." As he was praying, I began to tell God that I was putting this situation in His hand because He told me I can trust Him to handle me and all my troubles.

In less than fifteen minutes, that situation was ceased. This began to build my trust in God. He told me in His Word in so many different Scriptures that I could call on Him, lean on Him, and trust Him with any and everything. I gradually began to rely on Him rather than to rely on myself like I had done for so many years.

"And call upon me in the day of trouble:
I will deliver thee, and thou shall glorify me."
Psalm 50:15

I had to learn on a daily basis to trust on Him, but most importantly, to trust in Him. I had to learn to trust His Word. I was studying the Bible on a daily basis, but I wasn't putting certain parts of what I was reading and studying into practice. But when the trials and tests began to come, I began to trust Him more and I had to realize that He was not like man. He didn't let His Son, Jesus, my Savior, go through such a harmful death so that He would hurt me. It was just the opposite. He died so I wouldn't have to be alone when I felt like I was.

Jesus will never leave you nor forsake you. He's with you all the time. When you're up, He's there. When you're down, He's there. All we have to do is look up!

"I will lift up mine eyes unto the hills, from whence cometh my help.
My help cometh from the Lord, which made heaven and earth.
He will not suffer thy foot to be moved:
He that keepeth thee will not slumber."
Psalm 121:1-3

CHAPTER 10

The Importance of Being Intimate with God

ON THIS NEW JOURNEY OF the new me in Christ, I had to learn a lot about how to walk circumspectly. There was a lot to learn, a lot to undo, and a mess to deprogram from my thoughts. Learning "how" was altogether another process.

In my own way of thinking, I thought I just needed to be saved, delivered, set free, sanctified, and be born again of His Spirit. But I did not know that this was just the beginning of my new beginning. I had a lot of issues that needed to be dealt with, and one of those issues was knowing that it was okay to let God love me. But I also had to love on God.

When you grow up in a non-loving home, as in the sense of real love, not conditional love … "if you do this then I will do that …" or bribing love, or even just right down deception of love … it's hard to be vulnerable in the aspect of loving someone like a true and Almighty God. To me, on the outside looking in, I didn't want to be hurt anymore. I didn't want to let my guard down all the way. I wanted to love on God, but those scars of my past were stronger in the beginning than me letting my guard down in this particular area of my Christian walk. I didn't want to get close to God because I was viewing Him like my earthly father and people in general.

Then God began dealing with me on how to allow myself to love in the right way and allow Him to love me. The Holy Ghost would wake me up and give me scriptures. One of them was:

"But cleave unto the Lord your God, as you have done unto this day."
Joshua 23:8

God wanted me to pursue and cling to Him on a deeper level than what I was doing. The first thing He wanted was for me to spend quality time with Him so I could get to know Him better. I started doing this and found that I was opening up to Him a little at a time.

But God wanted to be loved, too. As humans, we want to take, take, take, and receive, receive, receive, without giving anything in return. That's not the way the Lord designed us to be. I found that I was spending more and more time with God through prayer, Bible Study, and learning His ways and His thoughts.

"Every word of God is pure: he is a shield unto those that put their trust in him."
Proverbs 30:5-6

By the continuous studying of the Word of God, I learned to allow my faith to be built up. It taught me how to endure many situations that I couldn't endure before. It taught me that the Word of God is like a shield. It teaches me the right way and the wrong way. It's my map on how to get from Earth to Heaven. Hallelujah to the Lamb of God.

My next step was learning how to listen to His voice on a deeper level. He didn't want me to love Him in the shallow waters; He wanted me to dive in a little deeper. If we stay shallow, then we are robbing ourselves of what could and should be.

My husband, Deacon Jones, says, "Take the limitations of God." If we think about that, it rings true. How can we serve a God so big that even the Earth is His footstool, and think that we'll receive all that He has for us in the shallow parts? I thought about this Scripture:

"Now when He had left speaking, He said until Simon, 'Launch out into the deep.'"
Luke 5:4

When Simon Peter obeyed Jesus, that's when the transformation came about. That's when he saw just how much he needed Jesus. I began to make it my purpose to love on God. I found Him to be sweet, kind, and understanding. The more time I spent in His presence, the more I wanted to be.

There's a Scripture that says,

"Thou wilt shew me the path of life: in thy presence is fullness of joy."
Psalm 16:11

I also came to realize this: there's no way that one can continue to walk in holiness and learn of His ways without spending intimate time with the Lord. It's a must and it is necessary.

CHAPTER 11

Learning to Walk in My Healing

AS I BEGAN TO WALK in the newness of God, I began to realize that this meant I had to learn to walk all over again. Not in the sense of physically walking, but emotionally and spiritually. I had to remind myself that the traumas and emotional abuse I encountered most of my life were my crutches from the crippling years. I took time to reprogram my way of thinking and seeing the world and the people differently. The woman behind this mask had to see the world through the lens of God, and this was not easy to do. To learn to walk in my freedom of healing was a daily process. Scripture says,

"For I am the Lord that healeth thee."
Exodus 15:26

Sometimes when I would get in a slumber mood or those unwanted reminders of my past would creep back in my thought pattern, I would feel like I was beginning to paddle backwards to being emotionally stuck. As I continued to look at the word, "healeth," I began to wonder why it said "healeth" and not "heal" or "healed"?

I began to search this word out. I didn't get it. Until one day! I heard a message about weeping enduring for a night but joy coming in the morning (Psalm 30:5). The pastor explained why the word "cometh" had the "eth" on the end. He then stated that every time we see a word with an "eth" on the end, means it is continuous. The Lord, through this pastor, answered my prayer. He, said, "I am the Lord that healeth thee."

That let me know that sometimes when I get discouraged or have a moment of despair, it does not mean that I'm not moving forward! It means that my healing process means that I will forever be walking in my healing!

No matter what it is, no matter what circumstance may arise, God still has His loving arms around me. I don't believe when the Scripture says, *"That by His stripes we were healed,"* it's not just talking about physical healing. It was talking about whatever predicament we are in – in our life – those stripes He took are so that we can be made complete with wholeness of body, soul, and spirit.

"But he was wounded for our transgressions,
he was bruised for our iniquities:
And the chastisement of our peace was upon him;
and with His stripes, we are healed."
Isaiah 53:5

I went from "healeth" to being healed. Back and forth, over and over, until I got the concept of being healed! But the Holy Spirit let me know that no matter how many times I needed to be reminded that I was healed, He was right there to remind me.

"Therefore we are buried with him by baptism unto death: that like as Christ was raised from the dead by the glory of the Father, even so we also should walk in newness of life."
Romans 6:4

CHAPTER 12

Your Turn

MY PRAYER IS THAT SOMEONE gets healed, saved, and set free and allows God, my Lord and Savior, Jesus Christ, to break the chains that has held them back for years. If He can do that for me, He will do that for you! If you're not saved but are hungry to be changed from the inside out, God can and will do it for you!

> *"If thou shalt confess with your mouth the Lord Jesus and believe in thine heart that God hath raised him from the dead, thou shalt be saved. For with the heart, man believeth unto righteousness; and with the mouth, confession is made unto salvation."*
> Romans 10:9-10

And just like that, you are saved. Now, go read Acts 1:8 about the power of the Holy Ghost. All you have to do is ask God to fill you with His Power. Then read Acts 2:4.

Get in a Bible-Based Church

It's important to assemble yourself in a Bible-based church. Not one where they give their opinions on how they think you should live, but one where they agree with what the Bible says through the pages of Scripture. I realize there are online services now, but Scripture also tells us to assemble together.

> *"And let us consider one another to provoke unto love and to good works. Not forsaking the assembling of ourselves together, as the manner of some is; but exhorting one another; and so much the more, as ye see the day approaching."*
> Hebrews 10:24-25

You will find that like-minded people will help you to further your walk in the Lord. If you live in the Texoma area, consider Full Gospel Holy Temple in Denison. I'm not saying we are the only church going to Heaven, but I know we are one of them! It's holiness plus nothing!

I pray that God will lead you, guide you, and direct your path on your new life in Him. And remember that you are free. Stay free, walk free, and help someone else find this new freedom you have in Jesus

God bless you all.

For Regina Jones, making a conscious decision to obey God by speaking out about sexual abuse and abuse and traumas of any kind is a must. Through much prayer, fasting and studying God's word, she is able to focus on her future and not live in the yesterday. Life experiences from a child into her adulthood have blessed her to help those in need of emotional healing and difficult situations. Her wisdom and guidance come from the Lord Jesus Christ by being obedient to the call that He has commissioned her to carry out.

Regina Jones is a loving mother, grandmother, committed wife, and a dedicated servant of the Lord Jesus Christ. This memoir is to let everyone know that total deliverance and being set free from any bondage is possible.

www.ingramcontent.com/pod-product-compliance
Lightning Source LLC
Chambersburg PA
CBHW051150050726
47594CB00003B/1329

* 9 7 8 1 9 6 6 5 6 1 4 7 7 *